STREAMS

Also by Joseph Kent

White Wind

STREAMS

Joseph Kent

Foreword by John Brander

Sunlight Publishers

Some of the poems in this collection originally appeared in the periodicals *California State Poetry Quarterly* and *In The Company of Poets*. Others have appeared in *The New Poet's Anthology*, edited by Laura Harris and William Jabanoski, and *The Irreversible Man*, edited by John Brander. Grateful acknowledgment is made to the editors of these publications for their support, and for permission to reprint the poems.

Several poems have also appeared in a limited edition, *White Wind*, Sunlight Publishers, San Francisco, 1989.

First published in 1996 by Sunlight Publishers
Post Office Box 640545, San Francisco, CA 94109

All inquiries and permissions requests should be addressed to
Sunlight Publishers

Library of Congress Catalog Card Number: 95-70499
ISBN: 0-9623751-3-6

Cover photograph © 1990 by Darilyn Rowan
Set in Garamond Antigua by Stormy Maddux
Photograph of author by Barnett Addis
Epigraph: *Sri Aurobindo*

Printed in the United States of America by
The West Coast Print Center

Ignorance transmuted becomes light that leaps beyond wisdom and knowledge.

STREAMS

Streams of a new consciousness

Anywhere on earth
in lonely treks

of yearning
untold

hidden streams
colonize light

Bold seeds prophesy
the global

roll of silver
arcs or leaps

of superconscient
fortunes

Blood shines
Fertile souls

thrive
in wind

CONTENTS

EMERGENCE

PASSAGE

Foreword

Joseph Kent's second collection of poems, *Streams*, is an advance in consciousness and perception, a further transmutation of the mundane into a poetry that leaps beyond existence and knowledge into an integral fullness of spirit. The title poem of the collection states what the journey Joseph is embarked on is about: "Anywhere on earth/in lonely treks/of yearning untold/hidden streams/colonize light . . . ."

Each poem is a stream that Kent follows. A poet still rooted in this earthly world, he appropriates to himself the light, as well as delight or Ananda, of a higher world, in words he makes his own and ours. Poets before him, and poets to come, have sought, and will seek, to bridge the mundane world of our everyday existence and that other, more tenuous home of the spirit, of what is higher within us. What Joseph does is to take us from one level of consciousness to another, then back again, leaving in us, by the end of the poem, an awareness of the one transmogrified by the light of the other, thereby enriching our inner world.

Sometimes we are left with a sense of loss that, trapped in one world, we are unable to linger in the other for more than a few poetic moments of time. Yet, after all the poems have been read and digested, what is left is an anticipation that we, in this world, are capable of living in both simultaneously, that the worlds blend and harmonize, and that there is a whole, a spiritualization of flesh and a materialization of spirit and light into bone and blood.

> It was just after noon
> when I walked along the Charles
>
> a glow on my original face
> before I was born
>
> ("The Way")

And a silent prayer of homage
rose for the ordinance
of clouds

("Drought's End")

dreams in eidolons of Being
and Becoming

waxes in the play
of eternal streams

. . .

even in the streets
and workaday world

. . .

or going through traffic
to Maria's house

("Reflections")

The key poem, for me, is "Your Light." Joseph quotes Sri Aurobindo to introduce the poem. "The world is here to manifest the unmanifest." This poem expresses the poet's own philosophy as we near the new millennium, as well as an aspiration that is universal in its appeal, and one, I, for instance, share. The words resound:

Cling to your dream in the waking world
and the light of your being

midst the dim crowd or contrary time

Employ the tools of your bliss
with invisible help

The chief difficulty of writing a higher poetry is that the link between earth and spirit gets easily broken. Poets are left with only earth in his or her work, with vague traces, if any, to something higher, or else get so absorbed in the spiritual as to lose all connection with earth, especially our animal nature, and one is left in air, as it were, without a foothold in the real (from our earthly point of view) world. It is so easy for such spiritual poems to be too abstract, lack substance, the word devoid of agreed meaning, and the ideas to drift like clouds meaninglessly across the mind's sky. Poets like William Blake and John Clare have bridged both existences, and it seems Joseph Kent, coming from a more Eastern point of view, has also fused the two into one.

That Joseph Kent is able to integrate earth and spirit into his work is remarkable in that, unlike mystics of old, he lives and works in late Twentieth Century America, in an urban nightmare of mental and physical pollution, competing, as most of us have to do, in rat races of dog eat dog, where stress, illness and crime abound: "These are rooms/where we exist—a world/of society's rising ante/and sombre weekends/survive as if/by miracles/and jazz." Not only to function in such a world but to be sane, humane, and sensitive is an achievement to be marveled at.

In his poems, as I have tried to show, there is earth and spirit, a dance of the two, one changing into the other and back again. Earth, however, is earth. Spirit is spirit. And yet there are images which combine both and are both. Whether we know it or not, all of us, to varying extents, oscillate between the two, living somewhere in a space in between. Joseph's poems express truthfully the in-betweenness we live and often experience. The poems, in one sense, go back to the very roots of poetry itself, to man's essence, his perception and sense of what is. At the same time, the poems take us forward to a new time, one we haven't reached, where, strange to say, we can reach our beginnings, where we started out from before, as it were, the fall. Kent is ahead of his time in that he looks forward to seeing a more widespread acceptance in the Western world of man's dual nature, and that all of us, once re-integrated, can live in a more holistic fashion, more conscious of who we are.

Lastly, why these poems are significant for the reader, is that the poet, unlike most Eastern philosophers and poets, values *samsara*. Buddhists and Hindus, for instance, assert, probably rightly, that our world (*samsara*) is one of illusion (*maya*). But for the poet, it seems right that he or she values this *samsara* and *maya* for its own sake, while, at the same time, being cognizant of the *nirvana* or enlightenment that lies as an available possibility for anyone pursuing a spiritual path Eastern or Western; for, in the depths and heights of integral *Self*-realization, this *samsara* is truly *nirvana*, and *maya* a creative power and infinite delight of cosmic play or dance (*Lila*) of the *Divine*. In this connection, I refer the reader to the many poems of or about cities. Four cities, in particular: Boston, New York, Denver, and San Francisco. His life in these cities, especially San Francisco, which is now his home and where he has lived for more than half of his life, is rooted in a reality, a physicality and visceral sensuality as he knows and experiences them. People also appear, vividly, as integral parts of his day to day reality. His cities become mine as he describes them. His friends, lovers, acquaintances, strangers, and crowds are those, in my own life, I know and live with. In "In The Stream," for instance, Kent says:

> Uptown and downtown, Eastside and Westside.
> I was working as a roving waiter. And at lone studies.
> Plush places. Gypsy stints.
> Nights I traipsed the streets of Manhattan.
>
> In the New York labyrinth, my life swerved,
> a roller coaster of ups and downs.
> Up to the Bronx and Harlem, down to the Bowery,
> the Village, Wall Street, and Lower East Side, or to Jersey.

While in "Ananda," a poem with a San Francisco setting:

> The Divine is everywhere. Grey days
> in this urban pearl of city enterprises
>
> that rise like helium balloons
> in the tiger light of August.
>
> Night brings imaginarium.
> Passion flight. Strands
>
> of white light over the bay . . .
> Starry tides.

In "Dharma Moon":

> The pleasure of sipping burgundy in San Francisco
> at an open air café in North Beach
>
> or on a starry night in the piazza
> at the Embarcadero
>
> That August moon swoons

For me, from a personal point of view, what I remember most is the mood of the poems. San Francisco is, more than any other city, my hometown, in that I was born there, grew up there (partly), and returned there to study and work, as well as write. It is Joseph's authenticity of description that takes hold of me. I am, indeed, held, and whatever it is holding me hasn't yet let go. And why would I want it to let go?

John Brander

On the shores of endless worlds children play.
—Rabindranath Tagore

SPIRAL

AURORA

October. Our days unfold with a blaze
of leaves and this chill

on the coast, autumn spirits
suffusing land and sea. The ancient seasons

turn, cosmos in flux, galaxies
in flight! To the horizon

stretch floral skies
pink and orange. Earth

forges on toward her epiphany
of new reality, spiraling

toward the oncoming panorama
of light, luminous efflorescence

for global hours, psychic days
in integral realms

in those fields
virgin beyond.

3

THE WAY

The Tao . . .

Mysterious and more mysterious—
The gate of all that is wondrous.

—*the Daode jing*

In my Zen paperback I pondered
the ancient Zen masters after the psychic awakening

To still the mind in eternal now

Twenty years old
in travel-worn clothes

workshirt faded blue
brown corduroy coat with ample pockets

I strolled under magnolias
in the morning mist

to the esplanade
along the Charles

The miracle of spring

Across the river loomed white colonnades
of the M.I.T. campus

On my left brownstone dwellings
overlooking the waters

Sails of the boat haven
fluttered in the wind

I let my thoughts rise
and dissolve

Poised on the green
my being slowed to a vacant calm

It was just after noon
when I walked along the Charles

a glow on my original face
before I was born

SOJOURN

Boston, New York, Jersey City, Chicago,
Minneapolis, Denver . . .

In how many rooms in American cities did I sojourn
in thrust of winter snow?

Here in my studio haven, these oyster white walls,
throng of books, paperbacks, sundry pictures
on knotty pine shelves

Walls with facsimiles of Monet's *The Hotel Roches—Noires at Trouvi*
De Niro's *Still Life with Spiral Chair*,
his *Moroccan Women*

Outside, voices, murmur of passing cars,
the streets, terrace chimes
and the garden, where thrush and gulls

mingle cries and song with the purl of neighbors' talk and melodies
Blue streaked sparrows fly this neighborhood cove

Cable cars rattle, clang and ring, climb to the Cathedral
or trundle down California

Near a tropical stelitzia of Oceania,
a giant bird of paradise,

a grey cat sprawls beside lavender
blossoms of mountain laurel

I lie on this sofa draped in green and blue flowers
of Indian spread cloth, books strewn
in piles on either side

Radio riffs flow from Miles, Thelonius
as a scent of burning hearth

wafts in through the yard
to my sanctuary

ANANDA

The Divine is everywhere. Grey days
in this urban pearl of city enterprises

that rise like helium balloons
in the tiger light of August.

Night brings imaginarium.
Passion flight. Strands

of white light over the bay . . .
Starry tides. A city

drifts in streams
of other history. Far beyond

our cinema glitz. While in cafés
on rolling boulevards

we drink the wine of earth
in flower seas of bliss.

DROUGHT'S END

for Dick Brewer

After the showers and Sierra
snows and windrains had stormed the green forests

and fresh mountain reservoirs
we went out to clean streets
of the city

Asphalt avenues dried with the houses
and white buildings

Gardens thrilled in the clear air
as nature replenished her soil

The ocean swelled in ozone

And a silent prayer of homage
rose for the ordinance
of clouds

RAIN

Slow rainy afternoon
when the world
stops in melancholy

We seek solace
in calm distraction
or favorite music

Outside, the rain
reminds of nature's
vast efficiency, brings

reflections that groom
the soul

or stirs sombre
reverie of heart
and mind

Rain like those rainy
winter mornings

when I would descend
to the day's streets

to buoyant toil
in Manhattan

Now years later
in this December rain
on another coast

I reflect on the tenor
of those days

and the tone
of this one

The kind of day
that proclaims
the world

NATIVE CITY

The El races in the South End
over snowdrift roofs.

Those mornings on the way.

Stormy days or sultry
nights I tread the bourn

of silver cares on Washington
and Tremont, roam the grey

streets, rhythmic bars,
blue cafés, past glittering

marquees of stardust—Publix,
Paramount, Pilgrim, RKO,

Metropolitan, Shubert, Colonial,
Astor—through shivering Boston

alleys, windy lanes, boisterous
traffic, even as a child, to

Scollay Square. Our city
escapades. A bustling West End

and North End drift
in mist and waterfront

tiers. Those days
of swans on summer

pond. The Public Garden.
Stone kiosks and subway

nocturnes. Boylston
opening on Copley Square.

The Huntington trolley trundles
below the spires and vistas

of Mission Hill. The Riverway
blooms and the Fenway

ranges green in Back Bay, sails
open on the Charles and gulls

flutter over an esplanade
and estuary

in all seasons
of the coastal light.

WAIFS

In a Yellow Cab on a Sunday afternoon
the children wait

There is something in their mother's eyes
and tears

Ages seven, five, and three,
the two boys and little sister

of 25 Darling Street
on Mission Hill

about to embark to witche's
chill and a winter
of orphans

The waifs are leaving in the cab
as to a funeral

Who will heed their call
on the cold plain?

THE WOUND

Stifled flower, child of the wound
wrought by the world,

you have seen the fear and chill
of the storm

in a glacial haze
of knots

like the wounded
anywhere, endured the blue

gloom, dwelling
in mourning

angst, your torn
petals yearning

for healing
light

for the wounded trying

15

JUNE HAVER ON A RAINY AFTERNOON

It was June Haver on a neighborhood
movie screen that rainy afternoon
in Boston when *Look For The Silver Lining*

appeared on theatre marquees
I was eleven years old
and her radiant beauty and talent
swept me away

June Haver, reigning blonde beauty
at *Twentieth Century Fox,*
had captured my heart
in her spell

Certain women truly do personify love
and the charms of Venus

I wanted to enter her world—theatre
and Hollywood

to know beautiful
June Haver

It was a long time ago

But what a transcendent
beauty

NORMA JEANE

Norma Jeane has gone off to be in pictures
after the heart wounds and dangers
of a quasi-orphan's itinerancy
with caretakers of the realm

Today she is charming
Ben Lyon, judicious head of casting
at *Twentieth Century Fox* studios

Little stoic on the periphery, mesmerized
waif of the glittering Saturday mornings
and afternoons in Grauman's Egyptian theatre

striving her way to incandescent fame
and a dreamer's blessing
on the threshold
of myth

EROS

Magnetic nights
when vital impulse
craves indulgence

and the heart
I go to Venus

and the fever
passes

to mild delight
above the tempest
of instinct
and Eros

In a blue room
she and I embrace
in early evening

or morning haze
when beauty glows

at an angle of soft light
and she smiles

blonde tresses
eyes blue, young goddess
in the shadows

and ardour
of desire

JACK'S SALON

Back then

Jimmy Doherty's rolling gold—passes one to Benny Folsom,
and it goes from Benny to Barry Borden once around
then to Jack at Jack Sheridan's place
off Huntington in Back Bay

Kim Loukas and I are drinking Jack's rosé tonight, talking Hesse
and Zen with pretty Vibke Lange as *Nirvana* flows
from the Jack Wilson Quartet on the easterly winds frequency . . .

Occasional guests stroll in and out through the evening
and early hours at Jack's salon on Symphony Road

Billy Barnum lounges on the deep burgundy sofa
scrawling poems, and rehearsing lines
in *The Changeling*

There's Virginia across the room rapt in *Latin Lace*
strains of Shearing

A full moon tonight and the bright waters
shimmer in Boston Harbor

Now it's Gloria Lynne on the waves
warbling *the night has a thousand eyes* . . .

as the night blooms a *Chagall*

SPIRAL

From luminous realms of *Sat-Chit-Ananda*
streams endlessly

descend in spiraling
planes of *Matter*,
Life, Mind

suffuse our fertile earth
in the cosmic drama
of Divine delight

cycle eternally
as the worlds unfold
to realms of higher being

turn on their spiritual axes
in every direction
of the cosmic play

JAZZ LOVE

for Jack Sheridan

The eternal impulse of the Spirit

flows through a jazz riff
on the radio

over epic lives

At the end of the dim corridor
in my apartment building

a light glows in the spirit
of Baudelaire

These are rooms
where we exist—a world

of society's rising ante
and sombre weekends

survive as if
by miracles

and jazz

MILES

Lyrical heart of the haunting refrain
Miles Davis birthed cool passion of the new jazz tone

in essence strains, moods blue, spontaneous polyrhythms,
stark breaks of intuitive reed

Blue beauty from the 52nd St. clubs
that sired fantasia

riffs, solo flares
in atmospheric

nuance of the sombre horn,
muted soul trumpet

Brilliant ensembles of blazing jazz odyssey,
atonal blue haze

Miles Davis, spirit Zen poet
of the jazz epiphany

INDUSTRY

On these stark streets
of guarded city

souls diverge
and wolves

stalk daily
under glaze of steel

At noon I pass
in tides of traffic

to the isle
in Times Square

Yellow cabs cruise
busy asphalt

Flutter of pigeons
on this open

strip surrounded
by neon

Over the canyons
the pensive

June day
fumes in twentieth

century enterprise
in the steamy sky

and pall
of tears

BLOOD DREAMS

Brahman jostles Brahman on these buses everyday
through troubled mornings
and evening rush

Industrial plumes are dreaming over the city
with its flickering loop
at dusk

Blizzard winds have obliterated
the highways to the north

In the unlighted labyrinth
of the steel pile
those hearts and heads
endure the hypothermic night

What brilliant evil
spawns this blight
of blood and dreams

The trip-wire tension
in cold streets

Dead replay of ignorance
to long star journeys

Swirl in my coffee
like the swirl of galaxies
over the poem
of the bay

ORPHANS

. . . beggars and homeless at every turn: people sleeping in doorways and on sidewalks around the city.

They weather the winds
by alms and chance

Those waifs, their stray
shoes, frocks, odds

and ends
strewn on orphan paths

After the streets
they pass on

to God
knows where

in the trials
and raw

night
of cities

SUNDAY

Sunday afternoon
as in India

Fog burned off
I gaze over

bay roofs
to the sea

over lines
of laundry

cries
of urchins
playing

bathe in
Spirit of East
in West

ponder worlds
manifest

arrivals
in Sun

spirits
in the wind

EMERGENCE

VIJÑĀNA

Viewing the brilliant horizon above
the trees, a wave

descends as a light
in the forest. In the woods

an inward man
ascends and descends, expands

and contracts in alternate
rhythms of discretion.

Twilight he fathoms
the night becoming

true day, ponders distance
for the realms of Sun.

He is at ease by the sea
and dwells in the forest,

his home in the stars.

EPIPHANY

All now is changed, yet all
is still the same. Savitri

The candles blaze . . .

They blossom out of dark
aeons. Is it not the divine
teleos?

Fire of life ascending into
day? *They* have

descended with gold
blessing, gifts of supramental

light unfolding in our world,
our life,
our moment—to fulfill

the brightest wish
of earth.

EMERGENCE

Out of this travail
issues our

divinity. Bliss
of diaphanous spheres

upper and lower
in the mix of the process.

Birth and death—
arrival or departure

in the east and west
north and south—

our transitional
birth and death.

Entering the Knowledge
we are born—

breathe
in *Vidyā*

live.

INTERIM

Appearing in the noon light, clear
winds from the sea

Eros sails the avenues
It is spring

The butterfly rises
and my heart . . .

SPRING POEM

Spring over the world. Girls in cotton
stroll the avenues and windswept
hills in every section

of this city in the sky. Those
kisses on balmy afternoons
and evenings of the Milky Way.

On boulevards young mothers
tend babies voyaging in blue
blankets toward the sea. Clothes

flutter in the wind of chimes
and balloons waft over the bay
to Oakland. Night and day

I return to familiar scenes
again and again.

AQUATIC

Those lights in fog on Golden Gate
brighten ochre and crimson.

Sun blazes gold into the sea.
This is cosmic séance

of marine afternoon, sunlight and air
and seaside play.

Months I walk this mobile
cove where gulls fly wind and blue

dolphins swim tides in swirl of day. White sails
glide this sound and coastal ferries

traverse the bay, their flags and flowing pennants
aloft on the cruise past Alcatraz . . .

Reposed on these aquatic malls
I can see those eucalypti and palms

that wave in ocean breezes
off the Pacific, the open sea

where spirit gulls soar
on the breast of the Eternal.

SUN BATH

The gleaming ocean. Up the coast a few miles
northeast of Boston, the loud waves crest
on a blue expanse of populous beach. White sand

burns in the sun. Billowing clouds above the flight
of those gulls that linger on the wing.
I think of Europe and the Orient. An ocean strip
of afternoon amusements delights the day.

Screaming frenzy of roller coaster
plummeting. Spell of beach carnival along the sea
charms this multitude of weekend bathers.

Over in the foamy surf
a little brother and sister splash
and dance in this sultry heat
of summer in July.

Early evening. Families
wend their way home. An orange sun
fades in the western sky.

DHARMA MOON

The pleasure of sipping burgandy in San Francisco
at an open air café in North Beach

or on a starry night in the piazza
at the Embarcadero

That August moon swoons
above the Bay Bridge

climbs over strands of lights
reflecting in waters below

The quiet on the moon
never leaves

Guests come
to the still field of the *Tao*

in this mall

They visit
You are there

From the moon you can see
ghostly aspects

see Earth
whole

ponder the peace
of infinity

delight
in all

A GLANCE

Love is eternal, its precious jewel beams
a diamond light

But finding our soul's companion
may seem impossible in this earthly
sphere of possibilities

On Sundays I would sometimes browse
the labyrinth of stalls and maze
of books at the *Green Apple*

I was alighting from a bus in San Francisco
that balmy Sunday afternoon

on my way back from the *Green Apple* bookstore
out on Clement at 6th and returning
to lower Nob Hill and home on Pine

As I stepped off the bus
at Van Ness, my gaze

embraced a wistful-eyed blonde miss, her lustre and radiant
aura recalling those gems of the Spirit
along the spectrum of Being

Diamonds glitter iridescent hues of the prism
when seen from varying angles

And when exposed to sunlight, they sparkle
phosphorescent, their brilliance heightened
by their cut and polish

How could I approach her in that flashing
instant of seeing?

And was it mere vital glitter or a lonely illusion
of my dazed imagination?

The bus carried her away and she went on in the day
to her life with an air of unconcern

leaving me to muse that save for some grace of fate
the pursuit of one's soul mate could go on forever
as futile and illusory

as the quest for rare diamonds in those distal regions
of Brazil, South Africa, or India
and that in this life we might never meet

even if I should roam to the ends of the earth,
travel the sands of *samsara*
among the precious *jivas* and the realms . . .

A MOMENT

Civic Center, San Francisco

Involved intensities of *Sat-Chit-Ananda*
suffuse these structures, grey buildings

that loom round a civic mall of Brahmic gardens
and a reflecting pool. Pedestrians

pass the homeless strays who linger here
off breezy avenues.

Beckoning in the astral clime
a world awaits its hour.

HOLIDAY

Our bus leaves the city in Nirvana
and rumbles to Golden Gate, a crystal
sheath of fog on the bay.

We hum the crisp
byways and bright woods of Marin
in autumn.

Miles the holiday hearth
crackles a scent

on this stretch
of rolling country

north in the grey
November hush
of afternoon.

FLARE

It is not your contemporary war

It will go on till our cities
meet eternity.

The battle flares
through the centuries. It

flames to the end
in another realm.

A transmutation.

It is the flare of dawn
and the night.

REALITY

Flicker of soul sparks
in the streets,

on the avenues, in homes
and cloisters of the land.

The *Tao* is dealing
cards—

yes and no
in the flux
of life—

in the furious winds
of fate.

INTIMATION

Nights when the great
coastal winds

of the jet stream
sink south

engulfing in fog
and cold showers

our bay enclave
I dwell

on nature's wisdom
and the ocean

of stars glimmering
beyond in vast

eternal distances of
mysterious space

and the future

It is then a white
ray of bliss

reminds
of Divine intent

in the cosmos
and the lure

of stars

STARRY NIGHT

(San Francisco)

The secret of happiness lies
in a creative fusion of the
unique and the cosmic.
   —Haridas Chaudhuri

Starry night in June

I climb to the silence
of my roof overlooking the bay.

Above, the stars . . .

Galaxies adrift. A sublime
arching over and under
of this cosmos.

And here, this terrestrial sphere—
this earth awaits release

of her silvery realities
to come.

THE SEASON OF LIGHT

A Christmas mist settles over the city
at dawn. It is the season of light.

The matrix race roves the earth
in travail with birth
of a new being.

Out there beyond
the barbarous comedy
of mind, glimmerings of the sacred

advance of Spirit involved
in flesh, the gene evolving

in light, bring *Magi*,
the children . . .

OMEGA

Maria and I stood on the open terrace
overlooking San Francisco Bay

as fog dissolved over the shoals and blue waters

"There's our sleeping princess," I said

I gestured toward an expanse of white sails
in evaporating mists, and distant rise of cloudscapes

"She's awakening," said Maria
as a grey haze yielded to sunlight

in a magic blaze like a world
transmuted in a golden field of joy,

the scene transmogrified in wondrous light

Maria smiled, her blonde tresses
radiant in the oceanic breeze

in a heavenly moment of illumined love
on the timeless terrace

while we lingered and gazed
toward the sunlit sea

PASSAGE

THE WILD GOOSE

The wayward wild goose flies the skies, free creature
of the air, strays from the usual

flock, expected habitat or formation
to travel the world over land and sea . . .

setting down in a safe spot
from time to time, a mountain

sierra or pond pine whose branches
waver and tremble when the migrant goose alights,

settles with difficulty on a limb, white
plumage of wide wings aflutter

to balance footing, adapt
in a solitary place or station, where

aloof and screened in sanctuary
it gathers strength for new flight

The wild snow goose yearns for a mate, flies
the void of odd ties, awkward

status of loose encounters
or passing flight of the alone

ORACLE

Ancient Chinese seers
divined by celestial light

yarrow stalks
or oracular coins
evoking

hidden lines of action
eternal wisdom
of *I Ching*

structured hexagrams
to commune with sea
and stars

to see the unseen
flux of yin
and yang

find glimpses in the now
in a jingle
of the toss

reflecting motion
change

reality
Tao

IN THE STREAM

The warmth of spring in New York!
Rough and tumble of winter!

Those salad days when I worked in clubs, cafés,
bistros, smoky cabarets.

In precarious tides of living, the scramble
to stay afloat. Swimming or sailing the streams.

Uptown and downtown, Eastside and Westside.
I was working as a roving waiter. And at lone studies.
Plush places. Gypsy stints.
Nights I traipsed the streets of Manhattan.

In the New York labyrinth, my life swerved,
a roller coaster of ups and downs.
Up to the Bronx and Harlem, down to the Bowery,
the Village, Wall Street, and Lower East Side, or to Jersey.

From skyscrapers I viewed the cosmic city,
panoramas of heights and misty spires
above the rivers and Long Island Sound.

In all kinds of weather I stood out
in the city. My life was weather
midst the towers and spires.

Juliet of the Spirits was playing at a Times Square theatre.
As I stood observing the glittering scene in December
on 42nd Street, an acquaintance handed over

a twist of Acapulco gold. A delusory pleasure,
though that winter afternoon, the glorious savour
of Fellini's film!

Christmas in New York brightens and glows,
a festival of lights. And in the holiday stores
in a child's face and voice
I encountered the joy of Christmas.

Difficulties piled up. In a mist of snow
covering Times Square at 3:00 a.m., as gaunt gargoyles
glared from building cornices, I headed toward the hospice
called Grand Central Station.

Life *de passage*, homeless trek through
the season of light and gloom . . .

But spring in New York brings thawing and relief.
Thank God!

Midst the Village tourist traffic, the night spots
on West 8th Street, the Eighth Wonder cabaret
pulsed with rhythms of the times. Here I, Zen wayfarer,
arrived in spring for the dancing beat of summer.

O resilience of youth!
O vast gyre!

And in my SoHo dwelling on Thompson Street off Houston
obliquely behind Saint Anthony's, I could hear
the old world priests harangue their flock in Italian
detonating through the neighborhood in Little Italy.

In the midtown sky, the Empire State Building
reached toward cold stars.

Washington Square lit up with canvases
along the green walks. The Village was bursting
with colors. Spin art, psychedelia, Pollock,
de Kooning, Kline.

It was June when I met Colleen,
who lived with her older sister on Staten Island.
The Staten Island ferry then was still only a nickel.

Seagulls trailed our ferry on the misty passage across the harbor
back to Manhattan to the Village.

The trees were changing in this metropolis. Changing in America
with motion across the land.

And on Thompson Street that fall I hoisted sails to navigate west
in the whelming streams of fate.

NODUS

You leave the labyrinth of childhood
and tangled scene of adolescence

with the thousand year stare

You look back on detritus
of forlorn neighborhoods,

neon passages of limbo bars,
electric maze of the weekend apocalypse,

those stone cathedrals ascending over
the city's asphalt intrigue,

cosmic Boston squares,
long New York avenues,

frantic subways,

wells of servitude,
studious bus terminals

You brood over indigent journeys through winter
impasse in snow and tears

over your native Boston of the El through the seasons
stirring haunted memories of years

you came up—gone loves

You recall the wild proletarian wine
of dancing nights,

boudoir sighs, epic strife,
mystic moons, blue vigils

You keep these forever
as you enter another sphere

adrift in the nodus
of the glitter of the old

and glimmer of the new
struggling to be born

ITINERARY

Night itinerary. I walk
this ocean city
in fog . . .

Above mist, sprawling heavens
of bliss.

Gusts of wind collide
against the grey stone

buildings desolate
at midnight on these streets.

An esteem for matter
sustains my delight
in a bulk of stone

and the spirit
of the sea.

San Francisco, March

SUNLIGHT

It is *That*, the *Vast*, *Vijñāna*
and the surge of undreamt of possibilities

breaking upon our world
in the sunlit dawn of integral awareness

fulfilling our evolutionary destiny. Aeonic
striving this side of the veil

climaxing in realities supramental
to which our world is heir, luminous

harmony of solar systems
in the starry vast

and the heat and bliss
of an eternal cycle.

YOUR LIGHT

The world is here to manifest the unmanifest.
—Sri Aurobindo

Cling to your dream in the waking world
and the light of your being

midst the dim crowd or contrary time

Employ the tools of your bliss
with invisible help

Sail new horizons in the wind
of the ideal

Hold the fulfilling thought
in the venture

Cherish the ancient one
the Divine

Know the Self

Unfold the future
in the now

Ascend to a luminous age
in new light

for the new millennium

EVOLUTION

. . . there will come other horrible
workers: they will begin at the horizons
where he has succumbed.

—Arthur Rimbaud

They assemble for the earth, aspire
toward Gnostic tiers

and Divine millennium

In a long cone of ascendence
they light the way

A new race
of cosmic

growth
ignites

the diamond
being

DIADEM

Now we transcend the dim amusements

and that which is most precious
becomes our focus.

It is from here
we shift to the future

beyond entropy and the cyphers—
those wiles of the Ignorance.

O waves of Divine Ananda! O dalliance!
O birds of bliss!

And under the mysteries—
affection for this world.

Our task of discovery,
our warm radiance.

O invisible ones! Pure rebels
in the mute advance!

Those unsung events
of mystic sadness—

the secret stories of the world—
the people of the depths—-the desperate

subway of our anguish.

A diadem of love floats above
the earth—the drift of

Christos, the Supramental dream.

O Agni!

We stand on the earth,
we greet the Supramental Sun.

Each pass brings new delight.
Each day in the dawn.

STORMY PASSAGE

This solitary evening I mull over
the slow conversion

Earth in life's blue mists
turns with invisible

light waking huge beauty
while the Four Horsemen

of the Apocalypse
flourish on a planetary binge . . .

storm in the cusp
of transit to a new age

It is a time of atrocities—rage,
madness, barbarous strife

This evening I want rest
and the silence of Brahman,

inner peace, starry space

Tat Tvam Asi

ACCEPTANCE

for Bina Chaudhuri

Slowly it happens, the marvelous
lifts earth, seeps through

to open sky, changes
world in archaic

shrinking, brings
health

of hemispheres,
continents, mirth

and wonder,
the stars—She

the Goddess
in infinite care

for her dwelling womb

in solar light
grieving

ONE EVENING

The *Golden Apples of the Sun* pulsed, swooned
a dwalm of colours and staccato
chirping in Chaplinesque

mirth as patrons
tasted the purple
juice, stumbled

against chairs. I pushed
away the table, asked
the time before I

floated
to the wood floor
in the rear of the café

descended to a nether world
in rite of shaman
dream

dissolved into vigil
presences. Symbols
rose and surreal streets!

I was light, ancient
pearl of soul in sun
and ocean of life . . .

In the delirious morning
of deliverance, paisley spectres
wafted in Dionysian winds

in the merciful hospital
and odor of ozone

till quiet afternoon
when I wandered
staid streets

in the polar light
and trace of the blitz.

Denver, January 1968

REFLECTIONS

Just as crystal beams vitreous light
so my being

deep within this numinous life
reflects in orbs
to cosmic seeing

dreams in eidolons of Being
and Becoming

waxes in the play
of eternal streams

in the Purnam Brahman of Time
and the Timeless

even in the streets
and workaday world

or on my way
to the marketplace

or going through traffic
to Maria's house

STREAMERS

The starry mysteries of our universe
pique our wonder

And perhaps the comets are our cosmic parents
bringing water, oxygen, organic molecules for Divine
design in the universal intelligence
of the spheres

Behind that girl over there waiting at the bus stop
with her green umbrella, at elliptical angles they orbit

destined for some great holocaust in the stella
stadia and primordial energy of *Prakriti*

Comets streaking light
in a golden glow of creation

We see them flaring in the night sky, aeonic
wanderers orbiting toward the Sun, transiting

the stratosphere of our heavens, streaming
from the unknown

like the blazing travelers that created oceans
long ago

THE CALL

Om Purno Ham Visiva Prem ["I am existence
being in its integral fullness, the spirit
of cosmic love."]

—Mother's Mantra

Lotuses of light

on the other side
and here

Urgency up
beyond the veil

The Grace
in acceptance

Critical mass
rising

in plastic
ascent

The descent
in surrender

to blossoming
and release

The Divine
earth

GALE

It is the candle

of your peace flickering
with the *presence*

in your heart of hearts

the *grace*
descending

the embrace
of the *Divine*

Om, shanti

MYSTERY

This life is miracle in mystery fathomed
and in this stream I follow clouds . . .

Today the sun is playing
with wind and sea

Not far from Nirvana cafés and Zen tables
I probe these City Lights books in San Francisco
as I used to browze book stalls
in Boston and New York

I was preoccupied in those days
with metaphysical muses
and the mystery

What is life? The traveler treads the path
over miles of a lifetime—play of *shakti* weaving
a way through the maze of change
in the *maya*

We go through life oblivious of
the mystery of our being,

creatures of this surface world
thrilling in outer magic

as in wild times
of young dream
and vital adventure

And even if blessed with love,
our path weaves on, arduous
journey in solitary turns

for great distances forever
along the stream of time

where eternal lamps beacon
over reflecting waters
and geography of real dream

in passage through days and nights
of coping over the stones
and winding spans of atmosphere
in the stretch of hazards, joys, delight,

bad weather, and blizzards of grief
or sunlit hours in soft strains,
till by impulsions of inward sense and urge,
auguries of psychic change and bliss

in this life or others,
the journeyer travels the way
to invisible pointers

leading under the rapture of the vast
toward the horizon of the soul
and the mystery

ON THE THRESHOLD

It is getting late
toward the end of the twentieth century.

I rest beside the blue ocean.

I wait in this sea city
in touch with global news.

It is getting late
as we explore—

O progressive world of luminous release!

Is it not late on the threshold
of ascent?

CHINATOWN

The turn through Chinatown for the 2001st time
under the flare of mandarin lanterns, late blue neon
down this street lit by amber lamps

I leave the nexus of *City Lights* and nightly flight
of Broadway night clubs, Columbus bars, café jazz, where *Specs*,
Visuvio, *Tosca* serve up beer, wine, mixed spirits,

libations of social euphoria, amorous rhythms
in the glittering magic, electric *maya*, vital lure and spree
of Barbary Coast and Babylon . . .

At the end of each vista off Grant
glimmering garlands of white light over the Bay

This morning 3:00 a.m. I pace the dragon path toward Old St. Mary's
through the wake of Chinese legends

Are there exotic pleasures, occult aphrodisiacs from another century,
slave girls and hashish in secret labyrinths?

Those tales of teleportation and divinations of *T'ai-i* magicians . . .
haze of opium off subterranean tunnels . . . myths
of miracle remedies and medicinal cures
by apothecaries of the outre in this kaleidoscopic

realm of oriental visions, spiritual alchemy of Taoist
temples in Chinatown, Asian enclave dreaming so still
in the vigil world of this mystic hour

ARRIVAL

On arrival, they will follow
the bright flowering of earth

beyond these terrestrial
fears.

They will live radiant
of spirit.

And you will blossom
in light

on gentle days
with a friend

by the sea.

THE TIME OF KALI

It seemed as though midst the spiraling violence, the floods
and natural disasters and tumult of our time,
Great Mother *Kali* were at work.

In San Francisco police sirens sounded day and night
and blitz of media from different parts of the earth
told us of the rage of mean crime, tempers and feelings

at flashpoint, exploding vengeance of blind ignorance
and corpses afloat on the stormy
waters—primal energy of *maya* in disarray . . .

Beautiful San Francisco coped in anguish, her atmosphere
charged with an eerie air of dread at the prospect
of further tremors and cataclysm that October

shortly after the 1989 Loma Prieta earthquake
of Northern California—toward the end of the millennium.
The Tuesday quake registered 7.1 on the Richter scale

along the San Andreas Fault. The fifteen second temblor
struck at 5:04 p.m. Our bus rocked, the terrified
driver fled, and shocked passengers abandoned the trolley
on Van Ness Avenue at Jackson Street.

Did not Heraclitus say that strife is the father of progress?

The usual rush of traffic bustled on Van Ness Avenue
late that afternoon when I left the State Building at Civic Center
to board the 49 Van Ness trolley to Aquatic Park.

Now the Bay Bridge loomed across a radiant bay, steel deck
sundered in the wake of the fiery quake.

Like many beset cities the world over, dreamy
San Francisco had come under a dark cloud, a victim
to some dire force of our time.

City Hall faltered in disrepair, its Corinthian columns,
stone parapets, cornices and arches
buttressed by wooden beams, interior of California marble

and Indiana sandstone cracked in the terraced rotunda
under the vaulting dome.

And as we looked around the globe through television windows
to daily news broadcasts of global calamities,
some fierce sweep of ruin seemed to topple
the forms of our world like fleeting playthings . . .

Surge of barbarism and scenarios of slaughter and hate
everywhere—epidemic of fear and trauma and innocence
maimed in the disorder and chaos of worldly distress,
dissolution, and wild plague . . .

Treachery of blood and guns
in the killing fields, demonic desecration
in a blight of atrocities . . .

Terror of radiating vehemence, marauders, and murders
in a procession of carnage and cruelty, shock and waste,
and destruction in the valleys of hell . . .

Deranged assaults of child sacrifice in murky wars—bombs
and stray bullets spawning death daily in the dark
smoke and fire of tragedy . . .

Lethal weapons in the flare of explosive events and global
uncertainty—the heat of evolution stymied and fear
of annihilation in the stream of crises, virulent music,
and absence of higher value . . .

Mother *Kali* in the rising fires of transmutation, her divine
force impelling us toward the saving grace
of higher consciousness—beyond this restless
energy of violence and doom . . .

NOTES TO THE POEMS

Spiral • A Moment
Sat-Chit-Ananda: Pure Being, Consciousness, and Bliss.

Vijnana • Sunlight
Vijnana: Original comprehensive consciousness; knowledge of the One and the Many, by which the Many are seen in terms of the One, in the infinite unifying Truth, Right, Vast of the divine existence; divine intelligence or gnosis.

Epiphany • Emergence • Diadem
Agni: Fire; Fire of Sacrifice; the Fire-God; Flame of Divine Force; illumined will, Divine Will; Fire of human aspiration; psychic fire.

Agni is the divine force which manifests first in Matter as heat and light and material energy and then, taking different forms in the other principles of man's consciousness, leads him by a progressive manifestation upwards to the Truth and the Bliss.

Ananda: Delight, bliss, spiritual ecstasy, the bliss of the Spirit which is the secret source and support of all existence.

Ananda is the beatitude, the bliss of pure conscious existence and energy, as opposed to the life of the sensations and emotions which are at the mercy of the outward touches of life and Matter and their positive and negative reactions, joy and grief, pleasure and pain. Ananda is the divine counterpart of the lower emotional and sensational being. It is the secret delight from which all things are born, by which all is sustained in existence and to which all can rise in the spiritual culmination.

Christos: In humanity, the indwelling Divine essence, manifested in Jesus.

Supramental: The Truth-Consciousness. What *IS*. A higher spiritual principle than Mind, or Supramental Consciousness and Divine Gnosis.

Vidya: Knowledge, the consciousness of Unity. Unity is the eternal and fundamental fact without which all multiplicity would be unreal and an impossible illusion. The consciousness of Unity is therefore called *Vidya*, the Knowledge.

Dharma Moon • Oracle • Reality
Tao (pronounced Dow): The "ultimate, all-embracing reality, the unitary principle that underlies the phenomenal, that unites and activates the dynamic polarities of Yin and Yang—'The Way'."

"The Tao is the way things are and work, the natural order of things."

A Glance
Jiva: The individual soul manifested in the world.

Samsara: "Faring on, journeying, existence, 'transmigratory existence,' the phenomenal world essentially identical with nirvana."

Stormy Passage
Tat Tvam Asi: Thou Art That.

Streamers
Prakriti: Nature, executive nature, creative energy or force of nature, energy apart from consciousness. Primal matter of the universe.

Reflections
Purnam Brahman: "Purnabrahman is the concrete unity of the Transcendent Absolute (parabrahman), the Cosmic Divine (Isvara), and the unique Individual Self (jivatman), which may be regarded as . . . three fundamental and eternally real poises of being or modes of existence." From the standpoint of integral reality, the superconscient transcendent, the phenomenal world of cosmic universality—i.e., energy, time, evolution, change, relativity—and the creative individual, are all integrally real and creative aspects of the supreme reality— Purnam Brahman.

Mystery • The Time of Kali

Maya: The great cosmic illusion, the creative power of consciousness by which the world exists, phenomenal. The original creative Illusion.

Shakti: Force, Energy, the Consciousness Force of the Spirit.

Kali: The Divine shakti, the Dark Face of the Universal Mother, Mother of all and destroyer of all.

SOURCES

Some of the note explanations above are from the following sources.

Schuhmacher, Stephan, and Gert Woerner, eds.
The Encyclopedia of Eastern Philosophy and Religion. Boston: Shambhala, 1989.

Chaudhuri, Haridas. *Sri Aurobindo: Prophet of Life Divine*. 2nd ed. Pondicherry: Sri Aurobindo Ashram, 1973.

Glossary of Terms in Sri Aurobindo's Writings. Pondicherry, India: Sri Aurobindo Ashram, 1978.

Tyberg, Judith M. *The Language of the Gods*. Madras, India: Kalakshetra Publications, 1970.

Pandit, M. P., ed. *Dictionary of Sri Aurobindo's Yoga*. Pondicherry: Dipti Publications, Sri Aurobindo Ashram, 1966.

A Glossary of Sanskrit Terms In The Life Divine. (With Two Appendices) Pondicherry: Sri Aurobindo Ashram, 1952.

Streams was set in Garamond Antigua type by Stormy Maddux.

Printed by West Coast Print Center

ABOUT THE AUTHOR

JOSEPH KENT was born in Boston, Massachusetts. He grew up in Boston and environs. After an adventurous adolescence in the Northeast, he worked at jobs in Boston and New York and other cities across the United States. A graduate of the California Institute of Integral Studies, he now lives and writes in San Francisco. *Streams* is Joseph Kent's second published book. His previous book of poetry is *White Wind*.